CW00850669

BEA

DRAGON

A Complete and Succinct Pet Owners Beginners Guide Manual

August Benitez

TABLE OF CONTENT

Description   of Bearded Dragon

The bearded dragon lives as much as its name: Like a dragon, it's geared up with the armor of spiny reptilian scales, which consist of a "beard" of spikes underneath its chin that puffs up depending on its temper. There are 8 species of bearded dragons diagnosed these days, all of which can be affectionately known as "beardies."

Most of the most popular puppy reptiles, bearded dragons tend to be mild, inquisitive, and energetic at some point of the day. The vital bearded dragon, Pogona vitticeps, is the most not unusual species to have as a puppy.

Habitat

Inside the wild, bearded dragons' variety extends across a maximum of Australia. They generally decide on to paste to warm, arid regions: deserts, subtropical woodlands, savannas, and scrublands. In the Nineteen Sixties, Australia banned the export of untamed bearded dragons; however, they've been bred within the United States for decades for the puppy exchange, and they come in a selection of shade "morphs" not generally observed inside the wild.

A warm habitat is essential for bearded dragons. They're cold-blooded and depend upon outside heat assets to elevate their body temperature, which varies consistent with the temperature of their surroundings. They bask in the sun to warm them and can burrow underground to avoid extreme warmness and predators.

They're semi-arboreal and regularly may be found on fence posts and tree branches.

Weight loss program

Bearded dragons are not picky eaters. With their robust jaws, they are able to clench and crush difficult-shelled insects like beetles. As omnivores, they'll additionally go for leaves, plant life, fruit, and the occasional small lizard or rodent.

Behavior

The beard, which both women and men have, is an essential manner the lizards talk. Whilst threatened, a bearded dragon will open its mouth, improve its chin, and puff out its beard to make itself appear bigger. This show may also be accompanied via a hiss.

Bearded dragons also communicate with the aid of converting the color in their beards and bobbing their heads. A quick head bob may additionally signal dominance, whereas a sluggish bob and an arm wave is an indication of submission.

With a change of seasons, some bearded dragons may fit through brumation, a sort of hibernation, wherein they forestall consuming and handiest drink water sporadically. This dormant section usually occurs in the fall or iciness because the light modifications and temperatures drop.

Courtship and breeding

To trap the attention of a girl, a male bearded dragon embarks on a showy ritual of courtship, pounding his feet into the ground and waving his fingers and bobbing his head. The male will pursue the woman and bite the lower back of her neck while mating.

A woman bearded dragons are believed to have the unusual capability to shop sperm, which permits a few to lay separate clutches of 11 to 30 eggs from an unmarried mating.

The intercourse of bearded dragon embryos may be modified with the aid of the incubation temperature. If the temperature is unusually excessive while embryos with male chromosomes are growing, they will instead develop as girls. warmer temperatures for the duration of improvement also make bearded dragons slower rookies.

Chapter one: How to feed a Bearded Dragon

Considering that bearded dragons have the sort of tame demeanor, additionally, it is very clean to feed it as long as it's in the right health. Generally, bearded dragons will eat right out of your hand, or a bowl, similar to the way a dog will.

It's great to get your bearded dragon into a feeding habitual. As soon as your bearded dragon becomes accustomed to the ordinary it'll be anxiously waiting when it begins getting close to feeding time.

Bearded dragons require one-of-a-kind diets at extraordinary degrees of its lifestyles. The food necessities for a toddler bearded dragon are lots one-of-a-kind than an adult. Right here we will cross over the way to feed a bearded dragon at every degree of its life.

Feeding a Baby Bearded Dragon

A bearded dragon is considered to be at the child (or hatchling) stage from newborn to 4 or five months antique. This period during its existence is whilst the bearded dragon is maximum fragile. Its miles very important for the duration of this stage that it get hold of sufficient vitamins and vitamins.

The dimensions and amount of food given all through this era may be very important. Never offer toddler bearded dragons prey foods which might be large than its head. Providing insects which can be too big can reason the bearded dragon severe injury, or maybe be deadly.

Baby bearded dragons have a sizable appetite and could try to devour prey this is too large. They could without problems slip into paralysis, or die, if this takes place. Feed them pinhead crickets which might be not than one-half inch long, small fruit flies, and the smallest wax worms to be had. This may assist to make certain the toddler bearded dragon can well chew and digest its meals without any issues.

Attempt to avoid feeding a baby bearded dragon mealworms. Mealworms have a difficult outer shell that can be tough for the toddler to digest and will result in paralysis.

Toddler bearded dragons have a high metabolism and want to be fed smaller, more common food. Also, babies have extraordinary dietary needs than adults. An infant bearded dragon's eating regimen must encompass about forty to 60 percent proteins (from insect prey), and approximately 20 to forty percent plants.

Provide tiny bugs three or 4 times in line with day and finely chopped vegetables at the least 3 times according to week. Offering the finely chopped vegetables once in keeping with the day is most reliable, and could help the toddler collect a flavor for veggies. Keep away from overfeeding babies as this could cause obesity and long term fitness problems.

Feeding A Juvenile Bearded Dragon

A bearded dragon is taken into consideration to be a juvenile as soon as it reaches a while between five months and about 18 months vintage. Through now the bearded dragon has gained mass and a few fat reserves and can be fed less frequently. In case you feed a juvenile bearded dragon on the identical price as a toddler, it could come to be overweight and suffer health problems later in existence.

The ratio of insects to veggies will change as nicely. With juvenile bearded dragons, you need to reduce down the quantity of insect prey to at least one feeding in line with day, whilst vegetables have to be served at least 4 times in line with week. the scale of insect prey maybe a chunk large as well, but don't forget to no longer feed it whatever large than its head.

At this point, the bearded dragon can be supplied gadgets that had been off-limits to toddlers, such as mealworms. It's far recommended to only provide mealworms once or twice according to week. It is important at this level to start imparting your bearded dragon greater veggies, and slightly much less insect prey.

Feeding an person Bearded Dragon

A bearded dragon is taken into consideration to be a grownup once it reaches an age over 18 months vintage. At this level in its lifestyles, the feeding time table becomes plenty more subdued, besides for girls at some stage inbreeding.

An adult may be offered a bendy, balanced eating regimen of insects and veggies as soon as a day, to every now and then once every other day. Its miles nice to provide greater veggies and fruit at this factor in their life and fewer insects

The grownup weight loss plan ought to consist of 20 to 25 percentage bugs and 70 to eighty percent vegetables (almost contrary to a toddler bearded dragon).

Adult bearded dragons may be presented pinkie mice, canned dog meals, softened rabbit pellets, or even small lizards. These objects should best be supplied as occasional treats, and only offered once each three weeks to a month. Adults are very liable to obesity so maintain an eye fixed on their increased price and adjust the amount of food presented.

Nutritional supplements

Diet and calcium dietary supplements have to be given to bearded dragons at each stage in their existence. The majority of these dietary supplements are available in a powdered shape that easily clings to meals. There are some dietary supplements that come as a liquid which you drop into the bearded dragon's mouth.

Infant bearded dragons ought to receive vitamin and calcium (with diet D3) supplements with at the least to a few foods per week. Actually dust a mild coating of the supplements onto the baby lizard's food.

Juvenile meals need to be dusted with a large spectrum nutrition supplement as soon as consistent with week, at the same time as including a calcium/D3 supplement to 3 foods consistent with week.

Adult bearded dragons must receive a vitamin and calcium/D3 supplement once in keeping with week.

Chapter two: When and how to clean a Bearded dragon

How regularly ought to you bathe your bearded dragon?

There's no set rule for a way frequently you need to bathe your beardie, but usually, once a week must suffice. Normal bathing enables preserve your puppy safely hydrated. But, bathing isn't the only supply of hydration to your beardie. Inside the wild, bearded dragons regularly get enough moisture from the morning dew. The perfect frequency of bathing for a beardie in captivity depends on many elements, such as the weather situation, moisture level within the air, and what kind of water it liquids on an ordinary foundation. As an example, inside the summertime months, you probably need to shower your pet two or three instances a week.

Whilst have to you increase the frequency of bathing?

In sure conditions, you can need to bathe your bearded dragon greater often. As an example, if your beardie gets a skin disease, including parasite contamination, the vet may additionally suggest a day by day bathing agenda for your puppy.

How long sought to a beanie bathe?

Commonly, a bearded dragon needs to shower for around 20 minutes. If, however, your pet is dropping or stricken by constipation, then the vet may additionally suggest a longer bathtub time to your beardie. This may behalf of an hour or maybe a complete hour.

Steps to bathing your beardie

In terms of giving your beardie, a fun bathing enjoy, a bit of education in your element can go an extended way. Earlier than you start, maintain all of the essentials accessible. For example, you'll want a bath, warm water, a mug or cup, a thermometer, and a gentle towel. Once you are ready, comply with the below steps.

Step one: select the proper bathtub

To start with, don't use your very own bath to wash your beardie. it's far common for a beardie to defecate in the bathtub. Often, their feces may additionally include the bacteria salmonella. So, the usage of the identical tub exposes you to the threat of getting contamination. Preferably, you must have a separate bath to your reptile pet. Do not forget to decide on a mini tub with excessive aspects, so that they cannot escape from the bathtub whilst bathing. For child beardies, you could even use your kitchen sink.

Step two: clean the bathtub field

This seems obvious however make sure you smooth the bathtub with water and vinegar combination every time before and after a tub. Bearded dragons are very touchy to chemical substances, so it's miles always a very good idea to keep away from the use of any chemical cleaners, such as detergents and soaps.

Step three: Fill the bath with just enough heat water

Preferably, the depth of the tub water must be one inch or lower. Basically, the concept is to maintain just enough water for the beardie to swim. However, you don't want the water stage to pass your pet's shoulder so that it will experience the tub with none fear of having drowned. Additionally, it is vital to keep the temperature of the water between ninety and 99 range Fahrenheit. At this stage, you'll want to apply your thermometer to measure the water temperature.

Step four: area a rock in the water

A few bearded dragons love to swim within the water for the long term, even as others select taking small breaks even as swimming. Your task is to offer them a solid surface that allows you to get out of the water and climb onto a dry surface as and when they want. To that stop, do not forget placing a rock at one corner of the tub.

Step 5: put your beardie inside the water

Once the setup is prepared, now you can place your pet inside the water for a bathtub. At this factor, you should keep a near eye in your beardie to see if it's miles playing the system. If, but, your puppy looks confused or still no longer prepared for taking a tub, supply it some extra time to settle in. To help it study the situation, for instance, you could splash the water inside the bath. That must help your pet fathom what's happening and prepare mentally for the tub.

Step Six: permit the beardie to bathe for a while

Now which you've positioned your bearded dragon within the tub, your activity is to just monitor them from a distance. A few beardies start splashing across the water at once, even as others can also make the effort to get acquainted. In both cases, just watch them from a distance. You have to now not go away them unattended, as they might need your assist whenever.

Step Seven: clean your beardie

When your beardie climbs onto the rock, use a cup or mug to scoop water over it's again and tail. But, if your bearded dragon is losing, you may use a soft-bristle toothbrush to do away with any loose pores and skin from its frame. Even otherwise, a gentle rub down with the toothbrush might assist clean the alternative frame parts of your beardie, inclusive of the areas over its head, underneath its belly and chin. But, don't massage the tender areas, which include its eyes and fecal or urinary openings.

Step eight: Dry your dragon and put it back in the enclosure

After you have got taken your beardie out of the water, the next step is to dry it off with a gentle towel. You may use any towel so long as its miles easy and gentle. Next, put the beardie lower back into the terrarium and turn on the basking light. As soon as a bearded dragon receives out of the warm water, it can experience cold. Therefore, it is vital to give it the option of basking within the enclosure.

Step 9: clean up the bathtub

It is constantly an amazing idea to easy the bath right now after the bathtub. That manner, you can put off any germs or bacteria from the field proper away – not allowing them to stay returned and regularly infects the location.

What if the dragon poops within the water?

A heat tub frequently facilitates inside the bowel movement of bearded dragons. So, you can anticipate your beardie to poop inside the water whilst getting a bathtub. In that situation, you have to at once get rid of the poop before it could contaminate the bathtub water. As a facet notice, bearded dragons generally don't urinate inside the bathtub water.

Are you able to shower your beardie within the exterior?

The quick solution is – yes, you may. However, preserve in thoughts a few matters earlier than you make that selection. To start with, make certain the climate circumstance for your area is appropriate for taking the beardie to an outdoor tub. For instance, if the climate outside is extraordinarily cold, then giving it an outdoor bath might not be an excellent idea. Secondly, try and keep away from the use of any outside hose to bathe the pet. In case you nonetheless need to achieve this, as a minimum do now not use high water pressure. Every other trouble with the use of an outside hose is that it's miles almost impossible to manipulate the water temperature.

The way to pass approximately cleansing the beardie's habitat

Just cleansing your bearded dragon isn't enough. You should also regularly clean the terrarium. In addition to the day by day renovation cleansing, you have to additionally provide the beardie's enclosure a radical cleansing every week. As part of your everyday cleaning, consider eliminating the waste substances, any droppings and uneaten food from the enclosure. Also, exchange the consuming water and disinfect the water bowls day by day. Your weekly cleansing agenda should consist of cleansing the enclosure internal out, replacing the substrate if essential, and cleansing the add-ons.

Chapter three: Suitable Vitamins for Bearded Dragon

In contrast to their wild opposite numbers roaming the arid deserts of Australia, it isn't uncommon for domestic bearded dragons to be poor in vital vitamins. Luckily, with the aid of genuinely knowing the first-class vitamins bearded dragon professionals swear with the aid of, you could speedy get your puppy back into tip pinnacle form!

In this newsletter, we are able to be focusing particularly on the subsequent 4 vitamins/minerals:

Calcium

Vitamin D3

Diet A

Multi-vitamins

Now, whilst this list may additionally seem overwhelming, please do now not be intimidated! Its miles incredibly not going you'll want to supplement your beardie's food regimen with five unique products

As an instance, maximum bearded dragons could make enough nutrition A surely by way of consuming meals rich in beta-carotene like bell peppers and squash. And on the subject of vitamin D3 nicely, there are positive husbandry setups that give enough of this that no similarly supplementing is required.

So, with that being said, let's dive deep into discussing all things vitamins for bearded dragons!

Chapter four: Bonding with the Bearded Dragon

Handling

Bearded dragons enjoy being dealt with even though they may now not trust you at first.

The more you manage a beardy, the greater it trusts you.

It gathers your heady scent and acknowledges each time.

Make sure you deal with your beardy the correct way to maintain it secure and build trust.

Check out our guide for how to pick out up a bearded dragon the proper manner.

If you don't have time to study this, comply with this brief version.

Flow your hand nearer slowly from in front of the reptile's face.

Scoop the bearded dragon up from under its belly.

Preserve all the lizard's limbs and tail supported.

Use one or arms as had to support and maintain the beardy in place.

When putting it down, ensure it's in touch with the ground before casting off your hand.

Give it a bath

Bearded dragons revel in baths.

It helps their skin, cleans them of bacteria, and helps them stay hydrated.

It's additionally a splendid way to bond along with your beardy.

Via having your puppy partner your scent with wonderful stories including bathing, you construct its affection toward you.

Take a look at our article on bathing bearded dragons for greater info or comply with the primary steps under.

Fill the tub with heat water as much as the shoulder top in your beardy.

Gently placed him in and permit him to adjust to the water.

Clean him via pouring water gently on his back, splashing his belly, and gently brushing as wished.

Play inside the water and spend time with him to soak up greater water.

Take out your beardy, pat dry with a towel, and put him inside the enclosure to bask.

Clean up the tub once you're accomplished.

Warning! Bearded dragons aren't to drink plenty of water or get their eyes moist.

Feed It by way of Hand

Whilst you feed your bearded dragon, it's vital to allow it to eat as much as it can in a 10-15 minute time frame.

This is additionally a time for bonding.

To build associations with meals and you feed your pet by hand.

This can make the reptile extra excited to see/smell you through the years.

Feeding by means of hand is easiest to do on plant life food.

The food doesn't squirm, chew, or jump.

Feed stay insects by means of hand, but a few might imagine that is gross.

Some roaches may also bite at you if you're not careful.

You oughtn't to do that the whole meal, however, a bit may additionally assist construct the bridge for bonding.

Caution! Keep your hands returned; bearded dragons can bite (although it doesn't harm a good deal or in any respect in maximum instances).

Calm down Your Bearded Dragon

In case you notice your bearded dragon is stressed, that is a brilliant opportunity for bonding.

The procedures for calming a bearded dragon additionally work properly for bonding all through this time.

Whilst calming your beardy, it's now associating you and your heady scent as a safe effect on its environment.

Play and explore

Take your dragon out and allow it to roam round exclusive regions (effectively).

Locate suitable toys and props for it to engage with.

At some stage in this time, ensure it is aware of your there.

This manner, it pals protection AND fun with you.

Through the years, it may even change its coloration as a manner to communicate with you whilst it wants to play and explore.

Be affected person and be there

None of that is carried out in the future or even a week, however consistently connecting along with your beardy over time can build the ones bonding associations.

Make sure you do those techniques as regularly as viable, especially with more youthful bearded dragons.